HILDA BOSWELL'S
TREASURY OF NURSERY RHYMES

Collins

CONTENTS

- What's The News?
- Lavender's Blue
- Old King Cole
- I Wish I Lived In A Caravan
- Ride A Cock-Horse
- Where Are You Going To?
- There Was A Crooked Man
- There Was An Old Man On The Border
- Two Little Kittens
- Mary Had A Pretty Bird
- Hector Protector
- A Farmer Went Trotting
- I'll Sing You A Song
- The Lion And The Unicorn
- Molly My Sister, And I, Fell Out
- The Man In The Moon
- Oranges And Lemons
- If All The World Were Apple-Pie
- There Was An Old Man With A Beard
- Hickety, Pickety, My Black Hen
- Hoddley, Poddley
- The Old Person Of Dover
- Little Girl, Little Girl
- Which Is The Way To London Town?
- There Was A Young Lady Of Bute
- The Swing
- Rock-a-bye, Baby
- When Good King Arthur Ruled This Land
- Diddle, Diddle, Dumpling
- Monday's Child
- Early To Bed and Doctor Foster
- Come Let's To Bed
- Jack Be Nimble and Lady-bird, Lady-bird
- Little Boy Blue
- Old Mother Hubbard
- Ba-a Ba-a Black Sheep
- Simple Simon
- Cock-a-Doodle-Doo!

I Had A Little Pony
Hark, Hark, The Dogs Do Bark
Pat-a-Cake, Pat-a-Cake
Mary, Mary, Quite Contrary
Humpty Dumpty
One, Two, Buckle My Shoe
Goosey, Goosey, Gander
There Was An Old Woman
 Lived Under A Hill
Bobbie Shaftoe
Hey, Diddle, Diddle!
Little Miss Muffet
Little Jack Horner and
 Little Polly Flinders
Polly Put The Kettle On
Hush-a-bye, Baby
Rub-a-dub-dub
Pussy-cat, Pussy-cat and
 Tom, Tom, The Piper's Son
The Owl And The Pussy-cat
Jack And Jill
Sing A Song Of Sixpence

Here We Go Round The
 Mulberry Bush
Little Tom Tucker and
 Georgie Porgie
I Saw A Ship A-Sailing
I Love Little Pussy and
 Multiplication Is Vexation
What Are Little Girls Made Of?
The House That Jack Built
Little Tommy Tittlemouse and
 Dame Trot
There Was An Old Woman
 Tossed Up In A Basket
The Three Little Kittens
Boys And Girls Come Out To Play
Tom He Was A Piper's Son
Curly Locks!
Little Betty Blue and
 See-saw, Margery Daw
A Dillar, A Dollar and
 Daffy-Down-Dilly
Jack Sprat

CONTENTS (Continued)

Ding, Dong, Bell
A Robin And A Robin's Son
The North Wind Doth Blow and
    Fiddle-De-Dee
Dickery, Dickery, Dock!
Three Young Rats
Pussy-cat Sits By The Fire
Ring-a-Ring O'Roses
Cock Robin
Some Mice Went Into A Barn
    To Spin
Hey Diddle Dinkety and
    Baby Bunting
This Little Pig

I Had A Little Hen
Little Jenny Wren
Twinkle Twinkle Little Star
One Misty Moisty Morning
The Queen Of Hearts
Little Bo-peep
I Had A Little Nut-Tree
There Was An Old Woman
    Who Lived In A Shoe
Three Blind Mice and Handy-
    Pandy
Mary Had A Little Lamb
Hot-Cross Buns
Wynken, Blynken And Nod

Wee Willie Winkie

WHAT'S THE NEWS

What's the news of the day,
Good neighbour, I pray?
They say the balloon
Is gone up to the moon.

LAVENDER'S BLUE

Lavender's blue, diddle, diddle,
Lavender's green;
When I am king, diddle, diddle,
You shall be queen.

Call up your men, diddle, diddle,
Set them to work,
Some to the plough, diddle, diddle,
Some to the cart.

Some to make hay, diddle, diddle,
Some to thresh corn,
Whilst you and I, diddle, diddle,
Keep ourselves warm.

Old King Cole

Old King Cole was a merry old soul,
    And a merry old soul was he.
He called for his pipe, and he called for his bowl,
    And he called for his fiddlers three.

Now every fiddler had a fine fiddle,
    And a very fine fiddle had he.
Tweedle, tweedle, tweedle-dee went the fiddlers,
    Tweedle, tweedle-dee.
Oh, there's none so fair, as can compare
    With King Cole and his fiddlers three.

I Wish I Lived in a Caravan

I wish I lived in a caravan,
  With a horse to drive, like a pedlar man!
Where he comes from nobody knows,
  Or where he goes to, but on he goes.
His caravan has windows too,
  And a chimney of tin that the smoke comes through;
He has a wife, with a baby brown,
  And they go riding from town to town.

Ride a Cock-Horse

Ride a cock-horse to Banbury Cross,
  To see a fine lady upon a white horse.
With rings on her fingers and bells on her toes,
  She shall have music wherever she goes.

Where are you going to

"Where are you going to, my pretty maid?"
"I'm going a-milking, sir," she said.
"May I go with you, my pretty maid?"
"You're kindly welcome, sir," she said.
"What is your father, my pretty maid?"
"My father's a farmer, sir," she said.
"What is your fortune, my pretty maid?"
"My face is my fortune, sir," she said.
"Then I can't marry you, my pretty maid."
"Nobody asked you, sir," she said.

There was a crooked man

There was a crooked man
      Who walked a crooked mile.
He found a crooked sixpence
      Upon a crooked stile.
He bought a crooked cat
      Who caught a crooked mouse.
And they all lived together
      In a little crooked house.

There was an old man on the Border

There was an old man on the Border,
Who lived in the utmost disorder;
He danced with the Cat, and made tea in his hat,
Which vexed all the folks on the Border.

Two Little Kittens

Two little kittens, one stormy night,
Began to quarrel, and then to fight.

One had a mouse and the other had none,
And that's the way the quarrel began.

"I'll have that mouse," said the bigger cat.
"You'll have that mouse? We'll see about that!"

"I will have that mouse," said the older one;
"You shan't have the mouse," said the little one.

I told you before 'twas a stormy night,
When those two little kittens began to fight.

The old woman seized her sweeping broom,
And swept the two kittens right out of the room.

The ground was all covered with frost and snow,
And the two little kittens had nowhere to go.

So they lay them down on the mat at the door,
While the old woman finished sweeping the floor.

Then they crept in, as quiet as mice,
All wet with the snow, and as cold as ice.

For they found it much better, that stormy night,
To lie down and sleep, than to quarrel and fight.

Mary had a pretty bird

Mary had a pretty bird,
Feathers bright and yellow.
Slender legs, upon my word,
He was a pretty fellow.

The sweetest notes he always sang,
Which much delighted Mary.
And near the cage she's ever sit,
To hear her own canary.

Hector Protector

Hector Protector was dressed all in green;
Hector Protector was sent to the Queen.
The Queen did not like him,
No more did the King;
So Hector Protector was sent back again.

A farmer went trotting

A farmer went trotting upon his grey mare,
Bumpety, bumpety, bump!
With his daughter behind him so rosy and fair,
Lumpety, lumpety, lump!

A raven cried "Croak!"
And they all tumbled down,
Bumpety, bumpety, bump!
The mare broke her knees,
And the farmer his crown,
Lumpety, lumpety, lump!

The mischievous raven,
Flew laughing away,
Bumpety, bumpety, bump!
And vowed he would serve them,
The same the next day,
Lumpety, lumpety, lump!

I'll sing you a song

I'll sing you a song,
Though not very long,
Yet I think it as pretty as any.
Put your hand in your purse,
You'll never be worse,
And give the poor singer a penny.

The Lion and the Unicorn

The lion and the unicorn,
Were fighting for the crown;
The lion beat the unicorn,
All round about the town.
Some gave them white bread
And some gave them brown;
Some gave them plum cake,
And sent them out of town.

Molly my sister, and I, fell out

Molly my sister, and I, fell out.
And what do you think it was about!
She loved coffee and I loved tea,
And that was the reason we couldn't agree.

THE MAN IN THE MOON

The man in the moon
came down too soon,
And asked his way
to Norwich.

He went by the south
and burnt his mouth,
With supping cold pease
porridge.

Oranges and Lemons

"Oranges and lemons,"
Say the bells of
St. Clement's.

"You owe me five farthings,"
Say the bells of St. Martin's.

"When will you pay me?"
Say the bells of Old Bailey.
"When I grow rich,"
Say the bells of Shoreditch.

If all the world were apple-pie

If all the world were apple-pie,
And all the seas were ink,
If all the trees were bread and cheese,
What should we do for drink?

There was an old man with a beard

There was an old man with a beard,
Who said, " It is just as I feared!—
Two Owls and a Hen, four Larks and a Wren,
Have all built their nests in my beard! "

Hickety, pickety, my black hen

Hickety, pickety, my black hen,
She lays eggs for gentlemen;
Gentlemen come every day,
To see what my black hen doth lay.

HODDLEY, PODDLEY

Hoddley, poddley, puddle and fogs,
Cats are to marry the poodle dogs,
Cats in blue jackets, and dogs in red hats;
What will become of the mice and rats?

The Old Person of Dover

There was an old person of Dover,
Who rushed through a field of blue clover;
But some very large bees stung his nose and his knees,
So he very soon went back to Dover.

Little Girl, Little Girl

Little girl, little girl,
 where have you been?
Gathering roses
 to give to the Queen.
Little girl, little girl,
 what gave she you?
She gave me a diamond
 as big as my shoe.

Which is the way to London Town?

Which is the way to London Town?
To see the King in his golden crown.
One foot up and one foot down,
That's the way to London Town.

Which is the way to London Town?
To see the Queen in her silken gown.
Left, right, up and down,
Soon you'll be in London Town.

There was a Young Lady of Bute

There was a young lady of Bute,
Who played on a silver-gilt flute;
She played several jigs
to her Uncle's white pigs,
That amusing
young lady
of Bute.

The Swing

How do you like to go up in a swing,
Up in the air so blue?
Oh, I do think it the pleasantest thing
Ever a child can do!

Up in the air and over the wall,
Till I can see so wide,
Rivers and trees and cattle and all
Over the countryside—

Till I look down on the garden green,
Down on the roof so brown—
Up in the air I go flying again,
Up in the air and down!

ROCK-A-BYE, BABY

Rock-a-bye, baby, thy cradle is green;
Father's a nobleman,
Mother's a queen.

And Betty's a lady,
 and wears a gold ring,

And Johnny's a drummer,
 and drums for the King.

When good King Arthur ruled this land

When good King Arthur ruled this land,
He was a goodly King.
He stole three pecks of barley-meal,
To make a bag-pudding.

A bag-pudding the King did make,
And stuffed it well with plums.
And in it put great lumps of fat,
As big as my two thumbs.

The King and Queen did eat thereof,
And noblemen beside,
And what they could not eat that night,
The Queen next morning fried.

Diddle, diddle, Dumpling

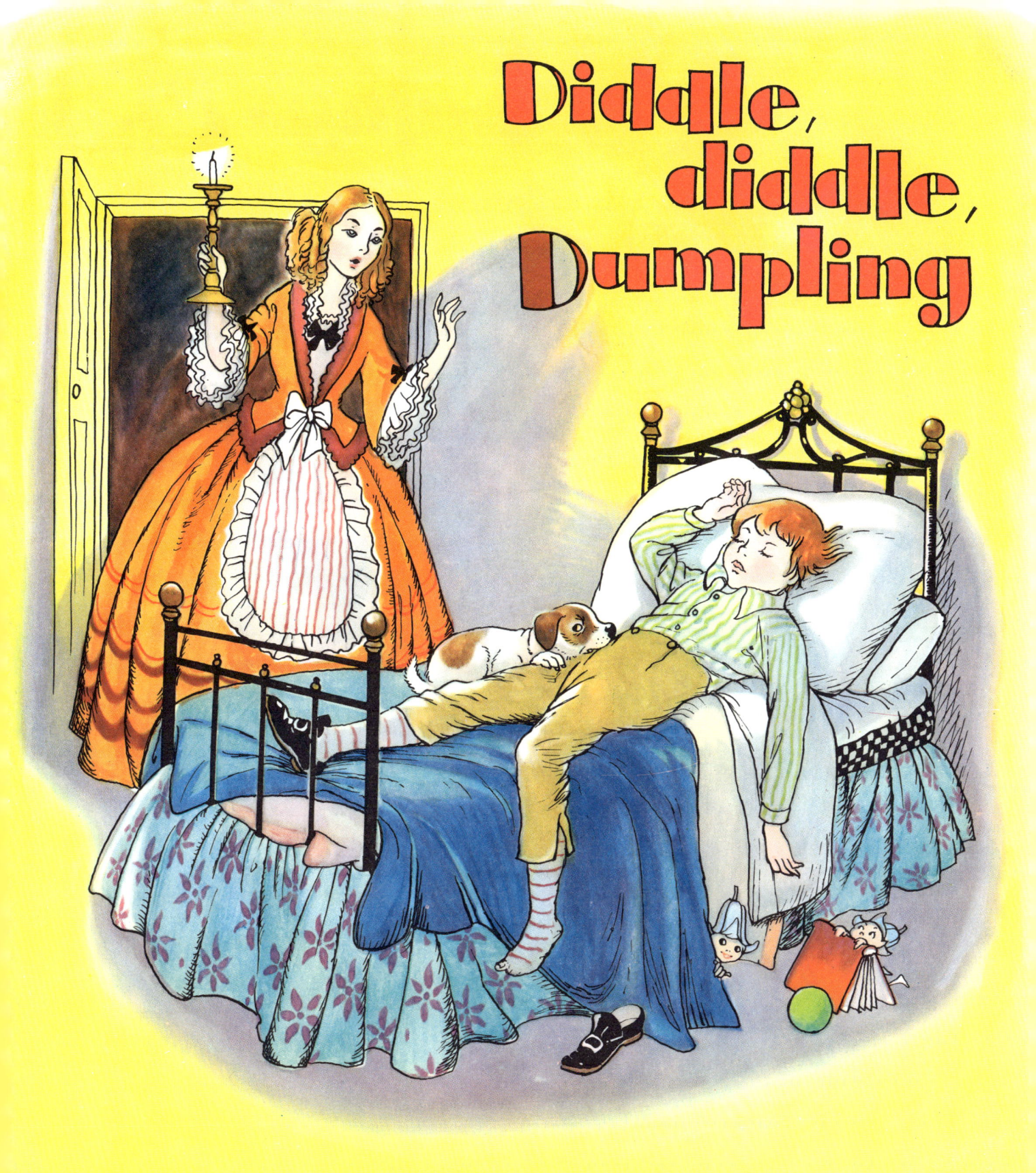

Diddle, diddle, dumpling, my son John,
Went to bed with his trousers on;
One shoe off, and one shoe on,
Diddle, diddle, dumpling, my son John.

Monday's Child

Monday's child
Is fair of face,

Tuesday's child
Is full of grace,

Wednesday's child
Is full of woe,

Thursday's child
Has far to go,

Friday's child
Is loving and giving,

Saturday's child works
Hard for his living,

And the child that is born on the Sabbath day,
Is bonny and blithe, and good and gay.

Early to Bed

Early to bed and early to rise,
Makes a man healthy,
wealthy
and wise.

Doctor Foster

Doctor Foster went to Gloucester,
  in a shower of rain;
He stepped in a puddle
  right up to his middle,
And never
    went
      there
        again.

Come let's to bed

"Come let's to bed," says Sleepy Head,
"Tarry awhile," says Slow.
"Put on the pan," says Greedy Nan,
"We'll sup before we go."

JACK BE NIMBLE

Jack be nimble,
Jack be quick,
Jack jump over,
The candlestick.

Lady-bird Lady-bird

Lady-bird, Lady-bird, fly away home,
Your house is on fire,
   and your children all gone.
All but the youngest,
   and her name is Anne.
And she has crept under
   the dripping pan.

Little Boy Blue

Little Boy Blue, come blow your horn,
   The sheep's in the meadow,
The cow's in the corn.
   But where is the boy who looks after the sheep?
He's under the haystack, fast asleep.

Old Mother Hubbard

Old Mother Hubbard
Went to the cupboard,
    To get her poor Dog a bone;
But when she got there
    The cupboard was bare,
And so the poor Dog had none.

    She went to the baker's
        To buy him some bread;
    But when she came back
        The poor Dog was dead.

    She went to the joiner's
        To buy him a coffin;
    But when she came back,
        The poor Dog was laughing.

    She took a clean dish
        To get him some tripe;
    But when she came back,
        He was smoking a pipe.

She went to the alehouse
   To get him some beer;
But when she came back,
   The Dog sat in a chair.

She went to the tavern
   For white wine and red;
But when she came back,
   The Dog stood on his head.

She went to the hatter's
   To buy him a hat;
But when she came back,
   He was feeding the cat.

The Dame made a curtsey,
   The Dog made a bow;
The Dame said,
      "Your servant."
The Dog said,
      "Bow-wow!"

Ba-a, Ba-a, black sheep

Baa, Baa, black sheep, have you any wool?
Yes, sir, yes, sir, three bags full:
One for my master and one for my dame,
And one for the little boy
                      that lives
                          down
                            the
                              lane.

Simple Simon

Simple Simon met a pie-man
    Going to the fair;
Said Simple Simon to the pie-man:
    "Let me taste your ware."
Said the pie-man to Simple Simon:
    "Show me first your penny."
Said Simple Simon to the pie-man:
    "Sir, I haven't any."

Cock-a-Doodle-Doo!

Cock-a-doodle-doo!
    My dame has lost her shoe;
My master's lost his fiddling stick,
    And doesn't know what to do.

Cock-a-doodle-doo!
    My dame has found her shoe,
And master's found his fiddling stick
    Sing doodle-doodle-doo!

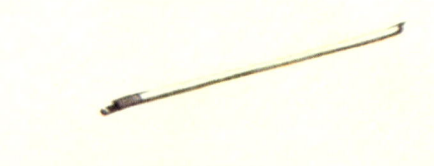

Cock-a-doodle-doo!
    My dame will dance with you,
While master fiddles his fiddling stick
    For dame and
        doodle-doo!

I had a Little Pony

I had a little pony,
        His name was Dapple-grey,
I lent him to a lady,
        To ride a mile away.

She whipped him, she lashed him,
        She rode him through the mire;
I would not lend
        my pony now,
        For all
            a lady's
                hire.

Hark, Hark, the Dogs do Bark

Hark, hark, the dogs do bark,
    The beggars are coming to town;
Some in rags, some in jags,
    And some in velvet gown.

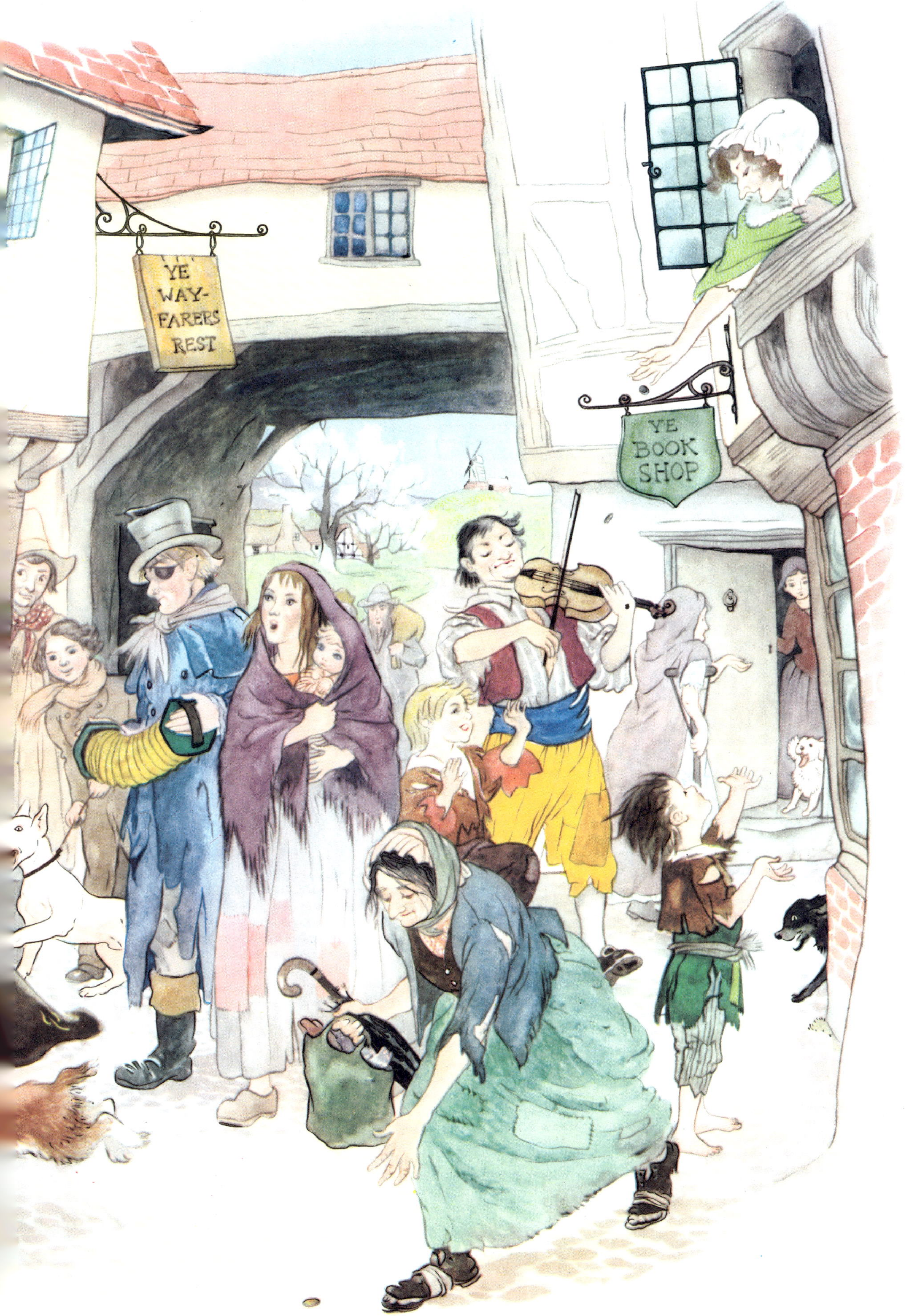
YE WAY-FARERS REST
YE BOOK SHOP

Pat-a-Cake, Pat-a-Cake

Pat-a-cake, pat-a-cake,
baker's man,
Bake me a cake
as fast as you can;
Pat it and prick it,
and mark it with B,
Put it in the oven
for Baby
and
me

Mary, Mary, quite contrary

Mary, Mary, quite contrary,
How does your garden grow?
With silver bells and cockle shells,
And pretty maids all in a row.

Humpty Dumpty

Humpty Dumpty sat on a wall,
Humpty Dumpty had a great fall;
All the King's horses and all the King's men
Couldn't put Humpty Dumpty
together again.

One, Two, buckle my shoe

One, Two, buckle my shoe,
Three, Four, knock at the door,
Five, Six, pick up sticks,
Seven, Eight, lay them straight,
Nine, Ten, the good fat hen.
Eleven, Twelve, dig and delve,
Thirteen, Fourteen, maids a'courting,
Fifteen, Sixteen, maids in the kitchen,
Seventeen, Eighteen, maids a'waiting,
Nineteen, Twenty,
my plate's
empty.

Goosey, Goosey, Gander

Goosey, goosey gander,
  Where shall I wander?
Upstairs, downstairs,
  In my lady's chamber.
There I met an old man
  Who wouldn't say his prayers,
I took him by his left leg,
  And threw him down the stairs.

There was an old woman

There was an old woman,
    Lived under a hill;
And if she's not gone,
    She lives there still.

Baked apples she sold,
    And cranberry pies,
And she's the old woman
    Who never told lies.

Bobbie Shaftoe

Bobbie Shaftoe's gone to sea,
Silver buckles at his knee;
When he comes back, he'll marry me,
Bonny Bobbie Shaftoe!

Bobbie Shaftoe's bright and fair,
Combing down his yellow hair,
He's my ain for evermair,
Bonny Bobbie Shaftoe.

Hey, Diddle, Diddle!

Hey, diddle, diddle, the cat and the fiddle,
The cow jumped over the moon.
The little dog laughed to see such sport,
And the dish ran away with the spoon.

Little Miss Muffet

Little Miss Muffet
   Sat on a tuffet,
Eating her curds and whey;
   There came a great spider
And sat down beside her,
   And frightened Miss Muffet away.

Little Jack Horner

Little Jack Horner sat in a corner,
   Eating his Christmas pie!
He put in his thumb,
   And pulled out a plum,
   And said, " What a good boy am I ! "

Little Polly Flinders

Little Polly Flinders
   Sat among the cinders,
Warming her pretty little toes;
   Her mother came and caught her,
   And whipped her little daughter,
For spoiling her nice new clothes.

Polly put the Kettle on

Polly, put the kettle on,
Polly, put the kettle on,
Polly, put the kettle on,
We'll all
have
tea.

Sukey, take it off again,
Sukey, take it off again,
Sukey, take it off again,
They've all
gone
away.

Hush-a-Bye, Baby.

Hush-a-bye, baby,
   on the tree-top,
When the wind blows
   the cradle will rock;
When the bough breaks
   the cradle will fall,
Down will come baby,
   cradle
      and all.

Rub-a-dub-dub

Rub-a-dub-dub,
   Three men in a tub,
And who do you think they be?

The butcher, the baker,
   The candlestick maker,
They all jumped out of a rotten potato,
   Turn 'em out, knaves all three!

Pussy-cat, Pussy-cat

"Pussy-cat, pussy-cat,
  Where have you been?"
"I've been to London
  To visit the Queen."
"Pussy-cat, pussy-cat,
  What did you there?"
"I frightened a little mouse
  Under the chair."

Tom, Tom, the Piper's son

Tom, Tom, the Piper's son,
  Stole a pig, and away he run.
The pig was eat, and Tom was beat,
  And Tom went roaring down the street.

The Owl and the Pussy-Cat

The owl and the pussy-cat went to sea
  In a beautiful pea-green boat.
They took some honey, and plenty of money
  Wrapped up in a five-pound note.
The owl looked up to the moon above,
  And sang to a small guitar,
" O lovely pussy! O pussy, my love!
What a lovely pussy you are, you are,
  What a lovely pussy you are! "

Pussy said to the owl, "You elegant fowl!
   How wonderful sweet you sing!
O let us be married—too long we have tarried—
   But what shall we do for a ring?"
They sailed away for a year and a day
   To the land where the Bong-tree grows,
And there in a wood, a piggy-wig stood,
With a ring on the end of his nose, his nose,
   With a ring on the end of his nose.

"Dear pig, are you willing to sell for one shilling
   Your ring?" Said the piggy, "I will."
So they took it away, and were married next day
   By the turkey who lives on the hill.
They dined upon mince and slices of quince,
   Which they ate with a runcible spoon;
And hand in hand on the edge of the sand
They danced by the light of the moon, the moon,
   They danced by the light of the moon.

Jack and Jill

Jack and Jill went up the hill
   To fetch a pail of water;
Jack fell down and broke his crown,
   And Jill came tumbling after.

Up Jack got, and home did trot,
   As fast as he could caper;
He went to bed and plastered his head
   With vinegar and brown paper.

Sing a Song of Sixpence

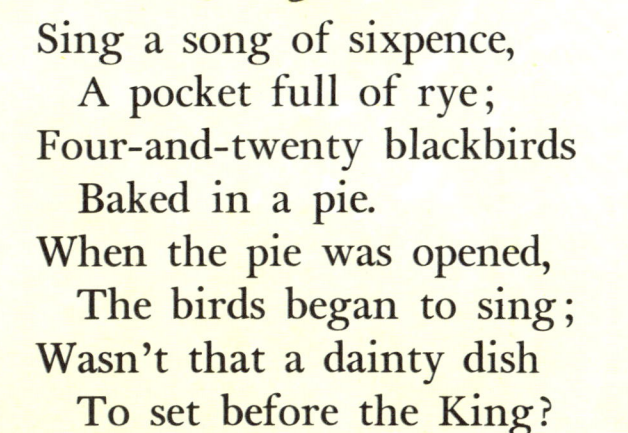

Sing a song of sixpence,
   A pocket full of rye;
Four-and-twenty blackbirds
   Baked in a pie.
When the pie was opened,
   The birds began to sing;
Wasn't that a dainty dish
   To set before the King?

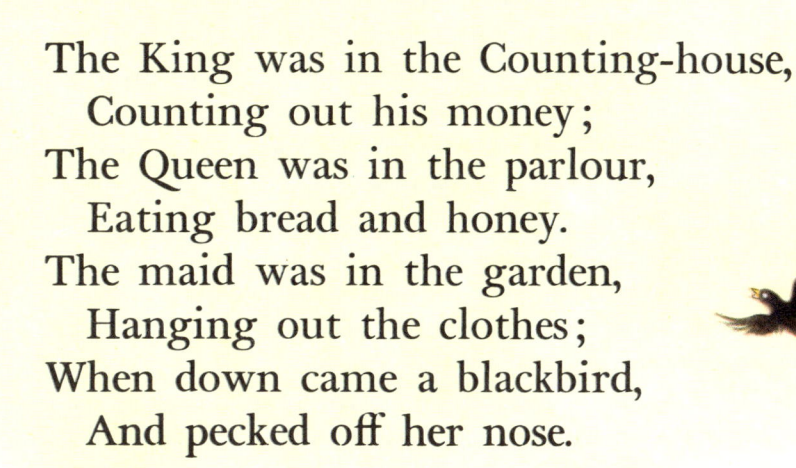

The King was in the Counting-house,
   Counting out his money;
The Queen was in the parlour,
   Eating bread and honey.
The maid was in the garden,
   Hanging out the clothes;
When down came a blackbird,
   And pecked off her nose.

Here we go round the Mulberry Bush

Here we go round
   the mulberry bush,
The mulberry bush,
   the mulberry bush;
Here we go round
   the mulberry bush,
On a cold
   and frosty
      morning.

This is the way we wash our hands,
Wash our hands,
wash our hands;
This is the way we wash our hands,
On a cold
and frosty
morning.

This is the way we wash our clothes,
Wash our clothes,
wash our clothes;
This is the way we wash our clothes,
On a cold
and frosty
morning.

Little Tom Tucker

Little Tommy Tucker
    Sings for his supper.
What shall he eat?
    White bread and butter.

How will he cut it
    Without e'er a knife?
How can he marry
    Without e'er a wife?

Georgie Porgie

Georgie Porgie, pudding and pie,
    Kissed the girls and made them cry;
When the boys came out to play,
    Georgie Porgie
        ran away.

I saw a ship a-sailing

I saw a ship a-sailing,
      a-sailing on the sea;
And, oh! It was all laden
      with pretty things for thee!
There were comfits in the cabin
      and apples in the hold;
The sails were all of silk,
      and the masts were made of gold.
The four-and-twenty sailors
      that stood between the decks,
Were four-and-twenty white mice
      with chains about their necks.
The captain was a duck
      with a packet on his back;
And when the ship began to move,
      the captain said,
        "Quack! Quack!"

I Love Little Pussy

I love little pussy,
 her coat is so warm,
And if I don't hurt her,
 she'll do me no harm.
I won't pull her tail
 or drive her away,
And pussy and I
 together will play.

MULTIPLICATION IS VEXATION

Multiplication is vexation,
Division is as bad,
The Rule of Three doth puzzle me,
And Practice drives me mad.

What are Little Girls made of?

What are little girls made of?
What are little girls made of?
Sugar and spice,
And all that's nice.
That's what little girls are made of.

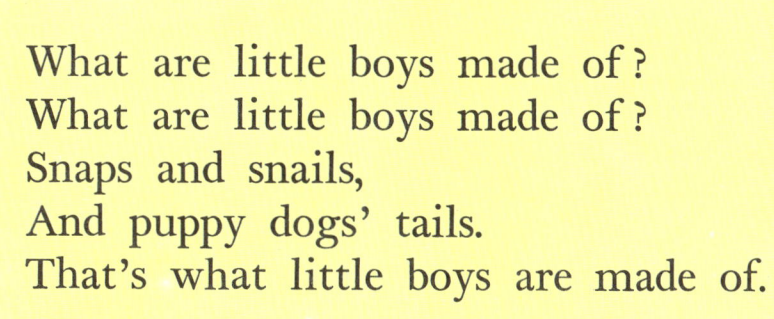

What are little boys made of?
What are little boys made of?
Snaps and snails,
And puppy dogs' tails.
That's what little boys are made of.

THE HOUSE THAT JACK BUILT

This is the house that Jack built.

This is the malt
That lay in the house
    that Jack built.

This is the rat
That ate the malt
That lay in the house that Jack built.

This is the cat
That killed the rat
That ate the malt
That lay in the house
    that Jack built.

This is the dog
That worried the cat
That killed the rat
That ate the malt
That lay in the house
    that Jack built.

This is the cow with the crumpled horn
That tossed the dog
That worried the cat
That killed the rat
That ate the malt
That lay in the house
    that Jack built.

This is the maiden all forlorn
That milked the cow with
    the crumpled horn
That tossed the dog
That worried the cat
That killed the rat
That ate the malt
That lay in the house
    that
        Jack
            built.

LITTLE TOMMY TITTLEMOUSE

Little Tommy Tittlemouse, lived in a little house;
He caught fishes in other men's ditches.

DAME TROT

Dame Trot and her cat,
Sat down for a chat,
The Dame sat on this side,
And Puss sat on that.

"Puss," said the Dame,
"Can you catch a rat?
Or a mouse in the dark?"
"Purr," said the cat.

THERE WAS AN OLD WOMAN

There was an old woman tossed up in a basket,
Ninety times as high as the moon.
And where she was going I couldn't but ask it,
For in her hand she carried a broom.

"Old woman, old woman, old woman," quoth I.
"Oh whither, Oh whither, Oh whither, so high?"
"To sweep the cobwebs off the sky."
"Shall I go with you?" "Ay, by and by."

The Three Little Kittens

Three little kittens they lost their mittens,
And they began to cry,
 "Oh! Mother dear,
 We sadly fear,
 Our mittens we have lost!"
"What! lost your mittens,
 you naughty kittens!
Then you shall have no pie!"
 Miaow, miaow,
  miaow, miaow,
Miaow, miaow, miaow, miaow.

The three little kittens they found their mittens,
 And they began to cry,
  "Oh! Mother dear,
  See here, see here!
  Our mittens we have found!"
  "What! found your mittens, you little kittens
  Then you shall have some pie!"
   Purr, purr, purr, purr,
   Purr, purr, purr, purr.

The three little kittens put on their mittens,
And soon ate up the pie;
"Oh! Mother dear,
We greatly fear
Our mittens we have soiled!"
"What! soiled your mittens,
you naughty kittens!"
Then they began to sigh:
Miaow, miaow, miaow, miaow,
Miaow, miaow, miaow,
miaow.

The three little kittens
they washed their mittens,
And hung them up to dry;
"Oh! Mother dear,
Look here, look here,
Our mittens we have washed!"
"What! washed your mittens, you darling kittens,
But I smell a rat close by!"
Hush! hush!—miaow, miaow,
Miaow, miaow, miaow, miaow.

BOYS AND GIRLS

COME OUT TO PLAY

Boys and girls come out to play,
The moon doth shine as bright as day.
Leave your supper and leave your sleep,
And join your playfellows in the street.
Come with a whoop and come with a call,
Come with a good will or not at all.
Up the ladder and down the wall,
A half-penny loaf will serve us all;
You find milk, and I'll find flour,
And we'll have a pudding in half an hour.

Tom he was a Piper's Son

Tom he was a piper's son,
He learned to play when he was young,
But the only tune that he could play,
Was "Over the Hills and
        Far Away."

Now Tom with his pipe
   did play with such skill,
That those who heard him
   could never keep still,
Whenever they heard him
   they started to dance,
Even pigs on their hind legs
   would after him prance.

As Dolly was milking her cow
 one day,
Tom took out his pipe
 and began to play;
So Doll and the cow
 danced the "The Cheshire
 Round,"
Till the pail was
 broke,
And the milk
 on
 the
 ground.

He met Old Dame Trot with a
 basket of eggs,
He used his pipe and she
 used her legs;
She danced about till the
 eggs were
 all
 broke.
She began to fret, but
 he laughed at
 the joke.

Curly Locks!

Curly Locks! Curly Locks!
    Wilt thou be mine?
Thou shalt not wash dishes,
    Nor yet feed the swine;
But sit on a cushion,
    And sew a fine seam,
And feed upon strawberries,
    sugar
    and
    cream.

Little Betty Blue

Little Betty Blue
Lost her holiday shoe,
What can little Betty do?
Give her another
To match the other,
And then she will walk in two.

See-saw, Margery Daw

See-saw, Margery Daw,
Jacky shall have a new master;
He shall have but a penny a day
Because he can't work any faster.

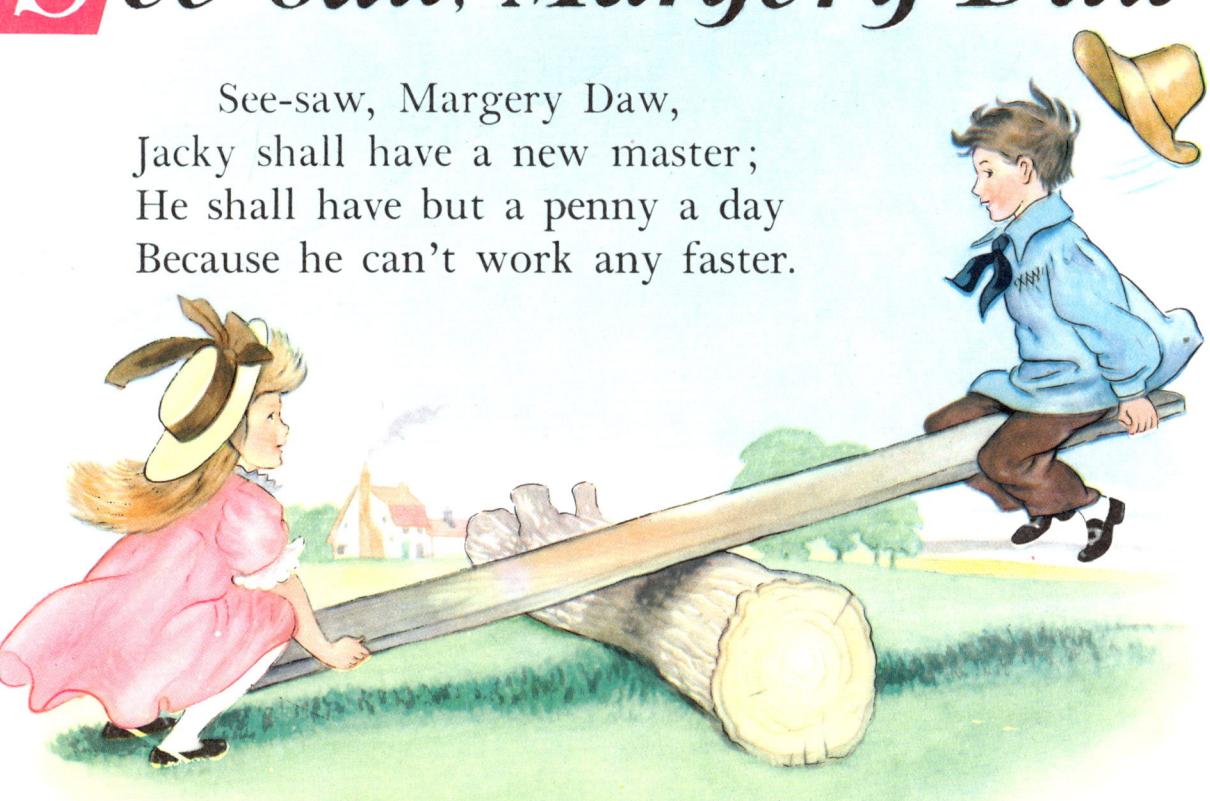

A Dillar, a Dollar

A dillar, a dollar,
A ten o'clock scholar.
What makes you come so soon?
You used to come
 at ten o'clock,
But now
 you come
 at noon.

Daffy-Down-Dilly

Daffy-Down-Dilly
 has come up to town,
 In a yellow petticoat
 and
 a green
 gown.

Jack Sprat

Jack Sprat could eat no fat,
    His wife could eat no lean;
And so b'twixt them both you see,
    They licked the platter clean.

Ding, dong, bell

Ding, dong, bell, pussy's in the well.
   Who put her in? Little Johnny Green.
Who pulled her out? Little Tommy Stout.
   What a naughty boy was that,
To try to drown poor pussy cat,
   Who never did him any harm,
But killed the mice in his father's barn.

A Robin and a Robin's Son

A robin and a robin's son,
Once went to town to buy a bun.
They couldn't decide on plum or plain,
And so they went back home again.

The North Wind Doth Blow

The north wind doth blow,
And we shall have snow,
And what will poor Robin do then, poor thing?
He'll sit in a barn,
And keep himself warm,
And hide his head under his wing,
poor thing.

Fiddle-de-dee

Fiddle-de-dee, fiddle-de-dee,
The fly shall marry the humble-bee;
They went to church and married was she,
The fly has married the humble-bee.
Fiddle-de-dee, fiddle-de-dee!

Dickery, Dickery, Dock!

Dickery, dickery, dock!
The mouse ran up
the clock:
The clock struck one
and down he run,
Dickery,
    dickery,
        dock!

THREE YOUNG RATS

Three young rats
  with black felt hats,
Three young ducks
  with white straw flats,
Three young dogs
  with curling tails,

Three young cats with demi-veils,
Went out to walk with two young pigs,
In satin vests and sorrel wigs.
But suddenly it chanced to rain,
And so they all went home again.

Pussy-cat sits by the Fire

Pussy-cat sits by the fire;
How should she be fair?
In walks the little dog.
Says, "Pussy! are you there?

How do you do, Mistress Pussy?
Mistress Pussy, how do you do?"
"I thank you kindly, little dog,
I fare as well as you."

RING-A-RING O' ROSES

Ring-a-ring-a-roses,
A pocket full of posies,
Atishoo-Atishoo,
We all fall down.

COCK ROBIN

Who killed Cock Robin?
I, said the Sparrow,
With my bow and arrow,
I killed Cock Robin.

Who saw him die?
I, said the Fly,
With my little eye,
I saw him die.

Who'll dig his grave?
I, said the Owl,
With my little trowel,
I'll dig his grave.

Who'll be the parson?
I, said the Rook,
With my little book,
I'll be the parson.

Who'll toll the bell?
I, said the Bull,
Because I can pull,
I'll toll the bell.

All the birds of the air
Fell a-sighing and a-sobbing
When they heard of the death
Of poor Cock Robin.

Some Mice went into a Barn to Spin

Some mice went into a barn
to spin,
Puss came by and popped her
head in,
"Shall I come and help you
to cut off your threads?"
"Oh no, Miss Puss. You might
snap
off
our heads."

HEY DIDDLE DINKETY

Hey, diddle, dinkety, poppety pet,
The merchants of London they wear scarlet,
Silk in the collar and gold in the hem,
So merrily march the merchant men.

Baby Bunting

Bye, Baby Bunting,
Father's gone a-hunting,
To fetch a little bunny skin,
To wrap Baby Bunting in.

THIS LITTLE PIG

This little pig went to market,

This little pig stayed at home,

This little pig had roast beef,

This little pig had none,

And this little pig cried,
Wee, Wee, Wee, all the way home.

I Had a Little Hen

I had a little hen,
   the prettiest ever seen,
She washed me the dishes
   and kept the house clean;
She went to the mill
   to fetch me some flour,
She brought it home
   in less than an hour.
She baked me my bread,
   she brewed me my ale;
She sat by the fire
   and told many
      a fine
         tale.

Little Jenny Wren

Little Jenny Wren
Fell sick upon a time;
In came Robin Redbreast,
And brought her cake and wine.

"Eat well your cake, Jenny,
Drink well your wine."
"Thank you, Robin, kindly
You shall be mine."

Jenny she got well,
And stood upon her feet,
And told Robin plainly
She loved him not a bit.

Robin he was angry,
And hopped upon a twig,
Saying, "Out upon you,
Fie upon you, bold-faced jig."

TWINKLE ★ TWINKLE ★ LITTLE ★ STAR

Twinkle, twinkle, little star,
How I wonder what you are,
Up above the world so high,
Like a diamond in the sky.

In the dark blue sky you keep,
Often through my curtains peep,
For you never shut your eye.
Till the sun is in the sky.

When the blazing sun is gone.
When he nothing shines upon,
Then you show your little light,
Twinkle, twinkle, all the night.

Then the traveller in the dark
Thanks you for your tiny spark;
How could he see where to go,
If you did not twinkle so.

One misty moisty morning

One misty, moisty morning,
      when cloudy was the weather,
There I met an old man
      clothed all in leather.
He began to compliment,
      and I began to grin,
How do you do,
      and how do you do,
And how do you do
      again?

The Queen of Hearts

The Queen of Hearts,
    She made some tarts,
All on a summer's day;
    The Knave of Hearts,
He stole those tarts,
    And took them clean away.

The King of Hearts
 Called for those tarts,
And beat the Knave full score;
 The Knave of Hearts
Brought back those tarts,
 And vow'd he'd steal no more.

Little Bo-peep

Little Bo-peep has lost her sheep,
  And doesn't know where to find them,
Leave them alone, and they'll come home,
  Bringing their tails behind them.

    Little Bo-peep fell fast asleep,
      And dreamt she heard them bleating;
    When she awoke, 'twas all a joke,
      For they were still a-fleeting.

Then up she took her little crook,
  Determined for to find them;
She found them indeed,
  But it made her heart bleed,
For they'd left their tails behind them.

It happened one day,
        as Bo-peep did stray
Into a meadow hard by,
Then she espied their tails,
        side by side,
All hung on a tree to dry.

I had a little nut-tree

I had a little nut-tree,
nothing would it bear,
But a silver nutmeg and a golden pear;
The King of Spain's daughter
came to visit me,
And all was because
of my little
nut-tree.

There was an Old Woman

There was an old woman who lived in a shoe;
She had so many children she didn't know what to do;
She gave them some broth without any bread,
And whipped them all soundly,
and sent them
to bed.

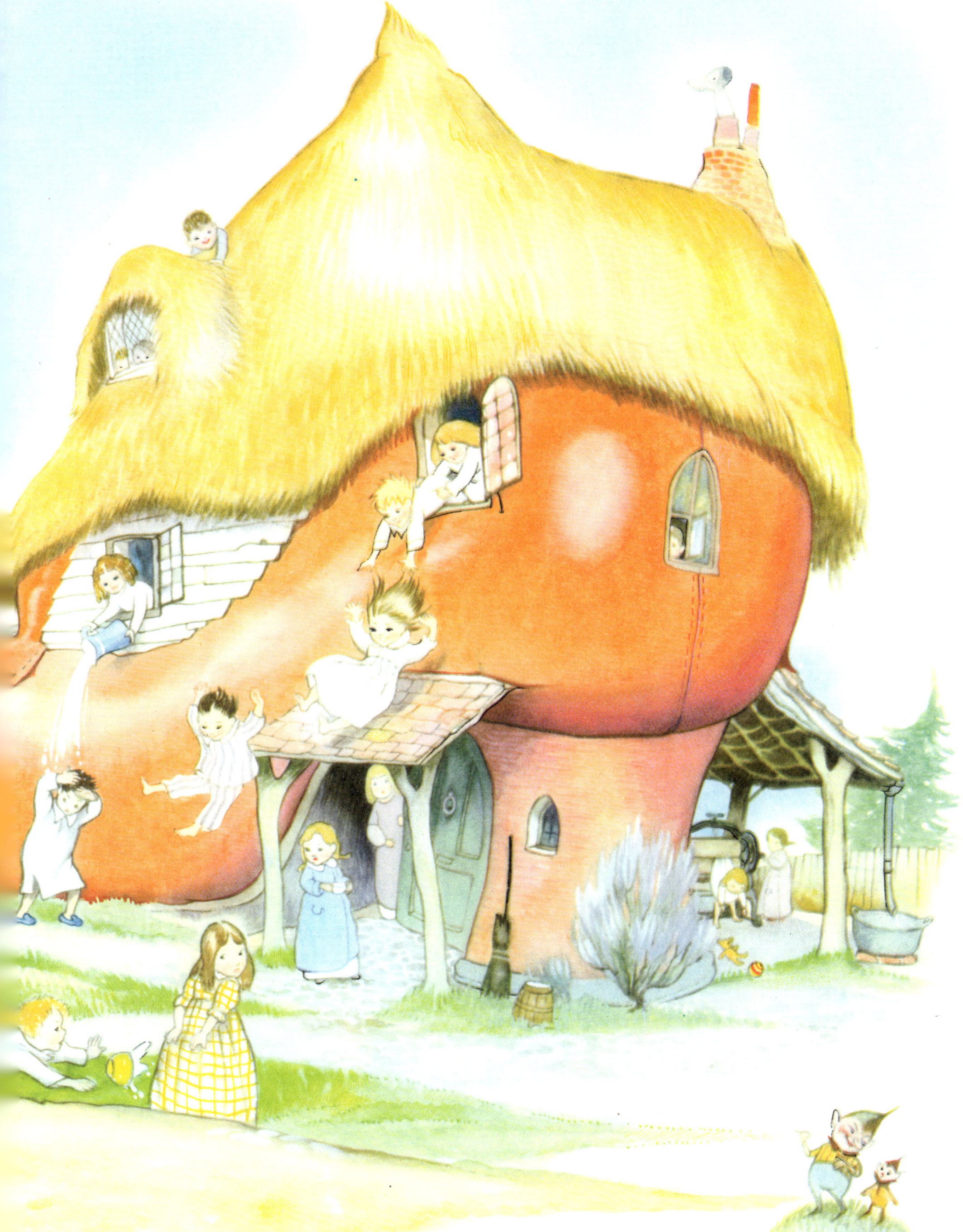

Three Blind Mice

Three blind mice, see how they run!
They all run after the farmer's wife,
Who cut off their tails
with the carving-knife.
Did ever you see
such a thing in your life 
As three blind mice?

Handy-Pandy

Handy-pandy, Jack-a-dandy,
Loved plum cake and sugar-candy;
He bought some at a grocer's shop,
And out he came,
    hop,
        hop,
            hop.

Mary had a little lamb

Mary had a little lamb,
   Its fleece was white as snow.
   And everywhere that Mary went
    The lamb was sure to go.

It followed her to school one day,
   Which was against the rule;
It made the children laugh and play
   To see a lamb at school.

And so the teacher turned it out,
   But still it lingered near,
And waited patiently about
   Till Mary did appear.

" What makes the lamb love Mary so? "
   The eager children cry.
" Why, Mary loves the lamb, you know."
   And that's the reason why.

Hot-Cross Buns!

Hot-cross buns!
 Hot-cross buns!
One a penny, two a penny,
 Hot-cross buns!
If ye have no daughters,
 Give them to your sons,
One a penny, two a penny,
 Hot-cross buns!

Wynken, Blynken and Nod

Wynken, Blynken and Nod one night
   Sailed off in a wooden shoe,
Sailed off on a river of crystal light
   Into a sea of dew.
"Where are you going, and what do you wish?"
   The old Moon asked the three.
"We have come to fish for the herring fish.
   They live in this beautiful sea;
Nets of silver and gold have we."
   Said Wynken, Blynken and Nod.

Wee Willie Winkie

Wee Willie Winkie runs through the town,
 Upstairs and downstairs, in his nightgown;
Rapping at the window, crying through the lock,
 "Are the children in their beds?
  For now it's eight o'clock."

ISBN 0 00 120302 9
First published 1962
This impression 1985
© Copyright Wm. Collins Sons & Co. Ltd. 1962
Printed and made in Great Britain
by William Collins Sons & Co. Ltd.

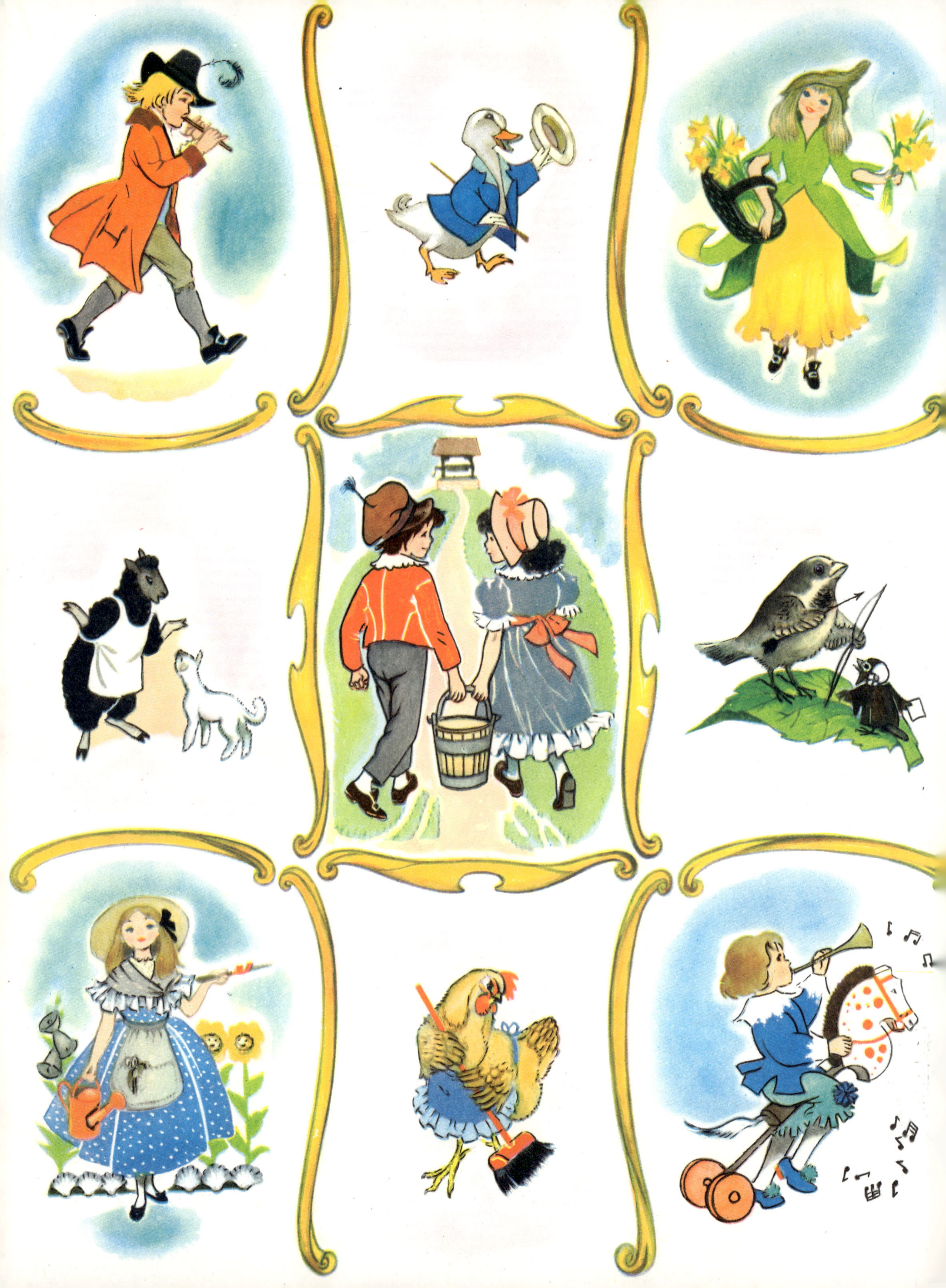